Let's Take a FIELD TRIP

A FIRE STATION
FIELD TRIP

by Isabel Martin

Consulting editor:
Gail Saunders-Smith, PhD

Content Consultant:
Lieutenant Jim Teed, Ret.
Engine Company 55
Boston Fire Department

CAPSTONE PRESS
a capstone imprint

Pebble Plus is published by Capstone Press,
1710 Roe Crest Drive, North Mankato, Minnesota 56003
www.capstonepub.com

Library of Congress Cataloging-in-Publication Data
Martin, Isabel, 1977– author.
 A fire station field trip / by Isabel Martin.
  pages cm. — (Pebble plus. Let's take a field trip)
Summary: "Simple text and full-color photographs take readers on a virtual field trip to the fire station"—Provided by publisher.
  Audience: Ages 4–8.
  Audience: K to grade 3.
  Includes bibliographical references and index.
  ISBN 978-1-4914-2096-6 (library binding) — ISBN 978-1-4914-2314-1 (pbk.) —
ISBN 978-1-4914-2337-0 (ebook PDF)
  1. Fire stations—Juvenile literature. 2. Fire fighters—Juvenile literature.
I. Title.

TH9148.M317 2015
628.9'25—dc23   2014032320

Editorial Credits
Nikki Bruno Clapper, editor; Juliette Peters, designer;
Gina Kammer, media researcher; Tori Abraham, production specialist

Photo Credits
Capstone Studio: Karon Dubke, 5, 11, 19; Corbis: Layne Kennedy, 17; Glow Images: DreamPictures, 21; iStockphotos: Graffizone, 9; Newscom: Eric Paul Zamora, 15, Michael Goulding, 13; Shutterstock: Cuson (middle right), cover, Denise Kappa, 7, Gemenacom (left), cover, Jim Parkin, 3, Joy Brown (top), cover, Kim Reinick, cover, 1, luchschen (middle left), cover, Mark Scott Spatny (background), 9, Monkey Business Images (right), cover, Pavel L Photo and Video, 2, 22

Note to Parents and Teachers

The Let's Take a Field Trip set supports national curriculum standards for social studies related to institutions, communities, and civic practices. This book describes and illustrates a class field trip to a fire station. The images support early readers in understanding the text. The repetition of words and phrases helps early readers learn new words. This book also introduces early readers to subject-specific vocabulary words, which are defined in the Glossary section. Early readers may need assistance to read some words and to use the Table of Contents, Glossary, Read More, Internet Sites, Critical Thinking Using the Common Core, and Index sections of the book.

Printed in the United States of America in Stevens Point, Wisconsin.
092014   008479WZS15

TABLE OF CONTENTS

A SPECIAL SCHOOL DAY

Today is field trip day.

Your class is going

to the fire station!

FIRE TRUCKS

Hear the siren wail!

Fire trucks park in the bay.

They have flashing lights
and loud horns.

Some fire trucks carry ladders. Ladders can reach the tops of tall buildings. Pumper trucks carry hoses and water for putting out flames.

FIREFIGHTER GEAR

Firefighters wear coats, helmets, masks, and boots. The heavy gear keeps them safe and dry.

LIFE AT THE FIRE STATION

Dispatchers tell firefighters how to get to a fire quickly. Dispatchers listen to radios, read maps, and answer calls.

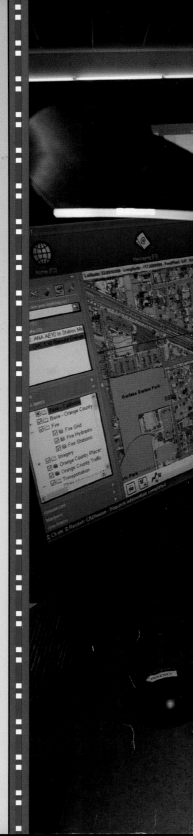

Firefighters spend time in
the training room. They learn
about new safety gear.
They learn to work together.

Firefighters exercise at

the station during the day.

At night they rest in beds.

A fire alarm could wake

them up at any time!

Firefighters cook meals in the kitchen. They eat together during breaks.

EVERYDAY HEROES

People at the fire station are heroes. They can be good teachers for a day.

21

GLOSSARY

alarm—a loud sound that warns people about an emergency

bay—the area in a fire station where trucks and other firefighting equipment is kept

dispatcher—a person who answers emergency calls and sends firefighters

field trip—a class visit for learning something new at a place outside school

gear—a set of clothing or equipment; firefighters wear heavy coats, pants, and boots called bunker gear

training—learning how to do a job

truck—a vehicle; fire stations use pumper trucks to carry and pump water; ladder trucks carry tall ladders to fires

READ MORE

Coppendale, Jean. *Fire Trucks and Rescue Vehicles.*
Buffalo, N.Y.: Firefly Books, 2010.

Kawa, Katie. *My First Trip to the Fire Station.*
New York: Gareth Stevens Pub., 2013.

Shepherd, Jodie. *A Day with Firefighters.*
New York: Children's Press, 2013.

INTERNET SITES

FactHound offers a safe, fun way to find Internet sites related to this book. All of the sites on FactHound have been researched by our staff.

Here's all you do:

Visit *www.facthound.com*

Type in this code: 9781491420966

CRITICAL THINKING
USING THE COMMON CORE

1. How do firefighters learn how to do their job?
(Key Ideas and Details)

2. Look at the pictures. What gear do firefighters use?
(Integration of Knowledge and Ideas)

INDEX

Word Count: 155
Grade: 1
Early-Intervention Level: 15